KU-417-577

MEDITERRANEO EDITIONS

Olive Oil

way of long life

Texts:
Stella Kalogeraki
archaeologist

Layout:
Vangelis Papiomytoglou & Nektarios Droudakis

Fotos:
Vangelis Papiomytoglou

Translation in English:
Alphabet Ltd.

Separations and Printing:
Typokreta

copyright 2002:
MEDITERRANEO EDITIONS, tel: +30 8310 20160

www.mediterraneo.gr

ISBN: 960-8227-00-3

Olive Oil

way of long life

CONTENTS

GREAT TASTES
BASED ON OLIVES & OIL

OLIVES & OLIVE OIL THE ROOTS OF AN ANCIENT CULTURE

A wall painting from the palace of Knossos showing an olive tree.

The olive in mythology

Mythology, historical accounts, traditions, and customs all provide evidence that olive oil has special properties, which over the centuries have been used in beauty, health, and medicinal products. The beneficial and often miraculous properties of the olive but mainly of its oil have helped it acquire a somewhat metaphysical nature and link it to rituals and religious worship.

Let us first take a look at the olive's place in mythology. According to mythology, the olive was brought to Greece by the Curetes, the giant-like, kindly deities who originated from Evia and who are known mainly from the time of Zeus'

This shield from the Idaen Cave shows the Curetes as winged gods surrounding Zeus.

birth when they settled in the Idaen Cave, clashing their shields loudly so the baby's cry would not be heard by his father, Cronus. Due to their introducing the olive, they are regarded as the benefactors of mankind. The idea and estab-

Ancient Athenian coin bearing the symbols of Athens: the owl and the olive branch.

lishment of the Olympic Games was even attributed to them, as it was they who first planted a wild olive tree from Crete in Olympia. The winner of the first race they held among themselves was crowned with a chaplet made from this wild olive tree, and ever since then, it has been the custom to crown Olympic winners in this way. According to another myth, the olive was given to mankind by the Goddess of Wisdom, Athena, who planted the first tree on the Sacred Rock of Acropolis, thus beating Poseidon and earning the right to protect and name the city of Athens. The sacred tree on the Acropolis is still in existence, forever linked to the history of Athens. Even when the Persians ruled the city and burnt the sacred olive tree, the following day the tree sprouted leaves again, revealing the goddess Athena's never-ending love for the city. According to another version of the same myth, the goddess Athena came from Crete and gave the sacred olive to the Minoans. This to a certain degree can be verified by the reference to the name of Athana Potnia on Linear B tablets found in Knossos. Thus it can be said that there is a link between the goddess Athena and the Goddess of Snakes in Minoan worship. Both the myths examined up to now show a direct or indirect relation to the olive as originating in Crete. Yet other myths link the olive to other regions of

This crater from 5th-century BC shows in the centre the protector of Athens, the goddess Athena, and the sacred olive tree growing on the Acropolis.

Greece, such as the Peloponnese where, according to one version, the first wild olive tree sprouted on the banks of the river Alpheus. In another

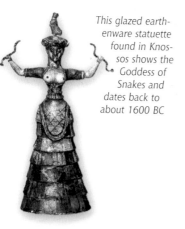

This glazed earthenware statuette found in Knossos shows the Goddess of Snakes and dates back to about 1600 BC

version, it was the hero of Greek mythology, Heracles, who brought the olive tree from the banks of the river Danube to Olympia, where he planted it and from there transferred it to Attica. The olive is also central to another important myth, that of the birth of Apollo and Artemis. When their mother, Leto, was searching for a place to give birth to her children who were fathered by Zeus, she went to the sacred island of Dilos. There she lay down in the shade of an olive tree, awaiting the goddess of childbirth, Eileithyia, to free her from the pains of labour and help with the birth. This olive tree was

This hydria from 4th century BC shows the contest between Athena and Poseidon for the domination of Attica. Winged Nike flies through the olive branch in the centre towards Athena, a sign of the Athenians' preference for the sacred tree, and consequently, the victory of the Goddess of Wisdom over Poseidon, whose trident brought about the creation of the sea, as shown by the dolphins depicted at the bottom of the vessel.

According to the myth, Heracles' club, which helped him win all contests, was made of wood from a wild olive tree growing near the Saronic Gulf.

considered sacred, and was looked after with great care on Apollo's island, Dilos. Apart from the myth relating to his birth, Apollo's name has also been linked to the olive through another myth concerning his son, Aristaeus. Aristaeus, son of Apollo and Cyrene, grew up in the area of the same name with his mother and the Nymphs who had undertaken his education. Apart from other things, he was taught how to produce cheese and honey, and how to engraft onto olive trees. Aristaeus was also a physician who dealt with epidemics and his treatment was based on olives and oil. In ancient times it was believed that Aristaeus was he who first had the idea of crushing olives to extract the oil. Perhaps this was when the olive came to be considered as a sacred and valuable

tree, and this in turn lead to it being widely cultivated and to the development of processes and techniques for extracting its precious oil. Besides, according to the myth, Aristaeus travelled not only within Greece, but also to Sardinia and Sicily where he shared his knowledge of oil production. In Sicily he was honoured as the god of olive cultivation. Apart from those myths featuring the olive tree, there are others in which the oil plays a leading role. Such is the myth according to which olive oil blended with other aromatic oils was considered the basis of the beauty cream used by the goddesses of Olympus.

All these myths and their different versions, apart from providing pleasure to the reader, show the importance of the olive tree, its fruit and oil in the ancient world. The tree was worshipped, as a whole culture grew up around both it and its products in relation to nutrition, health, daily life, worship, and economy.

Winged Aristaeus is depicted on this urn from the 6th century bearing gifts of oil, honey, and milk for men.

Olive tree from a wall painting in the Minoan Palace of Knossos.

The Minoan Years - Archaeological Evidence

According to archaeological facts, olives were being cultivated in Minoan times and indeed from the beginning of the 3rd century BC Olive stones and olivewood bear witness to its use in the daily lives of the Minoans.

Cultivation spread without doubt during the Mid-Minoan period, that is between 2100 BC and 1550 BC, as can be seen both from the many olive stones and the oil lamps found in excavations from this time. By the middle of the 2nd century BC, olive cultivation and its use in everyday life was widely spread. Crete must have been from that time an important olive-producing area with a developed economy, which without doubt benefited from the trading in oil in the Aegean islands and elsewhere.

During the same period, apart from olive cultivation for nutritional and economic reasons, a link between the fruit of the olive and idolatry began to develop. This is proved by idolatrous pottery in which were found olives offered to the deity. Apart from fruit offered in special rituals, oil was also offered in kernoi, the special round indented ceremonial pots in which a variety of produce was placed as

11

an offering of thanks and a gift to the deity. In addition, graves both from the Minoan and later years were often found to contain pots holding olives as gifts and supplies for the dead. From the

Conical cup with olives from the Minoan palace at Zakros. The excavator, N. Platonas, was impressed by the excellent preservation of the olives, which still looked fresh.

early years, therefore, the olive took on a leading role not only in everyday life and the economy, but also in idolatry and burial customs. The importance of the olive tree and its special significance for the Minoans can be seen in the art of the era. Both in pottery and jewellery, the olive tree often provided a source of inspiration for artists in Minoan Crete.

Archaeological finds of exceptional importance are those providing information on extracting oil from the fruit of the olive. In the archaeological area of Kommos on the south coast of Irakleio, two "presses" were discovered, consisting of circular stone bases with a groove around to collect the oil. The fact that this was an oil-producing unit is proved by the fact that in the same area, many olives and pots for transporting and storing oil were found. Apart from Kommos, stone oil-presses have been discovered at other archaeological sites, such as Faistos, Knossos and Vathi-petro in the area of Arhanes.

Another archaeological find providing valuable information on olive cultivation and production is the Linear B tablets found in Knossos, dat-

Stone vessels including some for oil pressing, found in one of the western storehouses in Faistos.

ing back to about 1400 BC. These tablets decoded by the Englishman Michel Ventris during World War II, depict ideograms bearing witness to the use of oil in everyday life, nutrition, idolatry, as well as in the economy and trade. It is

Linear B tablet from Knossos describing the existence of an olive-grove.

Ideograms in Linear B representing in turn: the olive tree, the oil and the fruit.

very impressive that three different symbols are used for the tree, the fruit and the oil. The same tablets refer to the existence of a palace olive-grove, while wild and cultivated olive trees are represented in a different way. It is highly likely that wild olive trees and their oil were used in pharmaceutics and perfumery.

Stone storage jars on the northern front of the central courtyard in the Minoan palace of Faistos.

The olive in Homer's epics

Rand oil in Homer's two eferences to the olive tree epic poems, on the one hand show how they were distributed at this particular time, and on the other hand, provide detailed information on their use in everyday life. The distinction between the wild and the cultivated olive is extremely significant, indicating the different use of each. Particular emphasis is placed on the use of oil in health, beauty, idolatry and burial customs. For example, the Iliad refers to the fact that Odysseas and Diomedes washed in warm water and then anointed themselves with oil. Afrodite anointed Hector's dead body with aromatic oil, and women rubbed their clothes with oil probably to make them shine. Excavation finds verify the widespread use of oil especially in burial customs, as in graveyards from the so-called "Dark Years", those that is corresponding to the time Homer lived and worked, have revealed not only pots for olives but also olives offered to the dead person for his final journey.

The aryballos is one of the most common types of pots found in graves of the Geometric years. These are perfume pots which according to one view were used as gifts accompanying the dead to the next world. Another opinion is that they contained the aromatic oils used to anoint the dead before burial. Homer in rhapsody 23 of the Iliad describes rosewater as one of the aromatic oils used to anoint the dead body.

The olive in classic antiquity and Roman years

Both the myths and the idolatrous rites that developed around the olive tree and its oil show the important position the sacred tree and its fruit held during ancient times. There is no doubt that this developed during prehistoric years and continued into classical and Roman times, contributing to what is known as the "olive culture" which was destined to affect the development of civilisation in Crete and the whole of the Mediterranean at all levels. The Ancient Greeks, following to some extent the ritualistic traditions of their forefathers, continued to treat the olive as a sacred and blessed tree and granted it an important position in their religious and idolatrous world. At the same time they exploited the benefits it could offer them in their everyday life. This can be seen in ancient Greek literature and texts whose writers refer unsparingly to the sacred yet practical nature of the olive tree. It is clear that during an-

cient times, knowledge concerning olive cultivation reached a high standard. The writer Theophrastus in his book "The History of Plants" provides a great amount of information on olive cultivation, planting and pruning. Harvesting olives took place in a way similar to that used today: ripe olives were either gathered from the ground after falling from the trees, or they were knocked from the trees with a pole, a process considered somewhat dangerous as it could damage the tree. After harvesting and collecting the fruit, the oil had to be extracted and this took place more or less as it is done today in three stages: crushing the fruit,

This black-figured amphora located in the British Museum shows the process of thrashing the olive trees.

pressing the pulp and separating the oil from the water. The fruit was crushed in "oil-mills", usually made of stone and of various types. This was followed by pressing the pulp in presses, which regardless of their type, consisted of a flat surface where the pulp was placed and a groove all round to collect the oil after pressing. The final stage was the separation of the oil from the water and other constituents, and this was carried out in a very simple way. The liquid was placed in a pitcher and separation took place automatically as the water and other constituents being heavier sank to the bottom and the pure oil stayed on the surface. Archaeological studies have shown that sometimes special pitchers were used for separation with a spout a little above the bottom which was opened to remove the heavy constituents at the bottom, and closed when only the separated pure oil remained in the pitcher.

The oil was then stored in large stone jars, which were kept in clean cool places. If the oil was to be exported, transported by ship, it was placed, like wine, in urns the bottom of which was not flat but pointed so as fit into special racks and thus travel in safety.

It is therefore clear that people in the ancient world not only had developed their knowledge of olive growing, but had also made progress in the development of technology concerning oil production. This was probably due to the fact

This pot today located in Boston depicts for the first time an oil press. One can see the wooden base where the sacks were placed and the lever which descended with the help of weights in sacks.

that producing oil was in many ways profitable and as already mentioned, provided a solution to many everyday problems. Firstly, it was a basic ingredient in cooking, provided lighting as fuel for lamps, and was a basic constituent in

Sharp-bottom amphora. Marine archaeologists often discover these amphora at the bottom of the sea, which shows that sea trading, product import and export, was flourishing in ancient times. These shipwrecks provide important evidence of prospering trade relations.

perfumery. It was also essential in beauty, health and of course medicinal products. The use of oil for anointing was widely popular in classical and Roman times when it was a basic "tool" for athletes, essential for strong muscles and a healthy body. More specifically, in order for athletes, and aristocrats too, in the ancient world to ensure their bodies

were clean, they rubbed themselves with oil, which was then removed with the help of a special metal tool, the strigil, along with dirt and sweat as well. Apart from being used as a beauty product, therefore, oil ensured physical well-being and cleanliness.

Historical evidence also points to the healing properties of oil. As we have seen, according to the myth, Aristaeus, son of Apollo and Cyrene, was taught by the Nymphs to cultivate olives and he also studied the healing properties of oil, mainly that of wild olives. However the first person to systematically study and codify the healing properties of oil was the father of medicine, Hippocrates. In his book "Dietetics and Therapeusis", he refers in length to oil and its importance to healthy development, while also mentioning many diseases that could be treated with olive oil, includ-

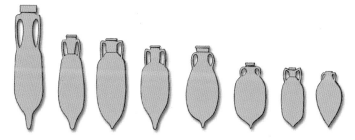

ing dermatoses, fever, poisoning, ulcers, etc. He also considered it beneficial in cases of miscarriage and to facilitate birth, as well as for healing wounds. Apart from Hippocrates, other ancient writers such as Plutarch and Ailianus refer to the healing properties of oil in the treatment of various ailments, not only in humans but also in animals.

Lamps and perfume cruets revealed by archaeological excavations bear witness to the extensive use of oil and its necessity for the development of all levels of culture, from the most practical to the most refined.

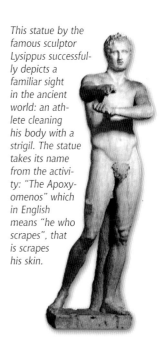

This statue by the famous sculptor Lysippus successfully depicts a familiar sight in the ancient world: an athlete cleaning his body with a strigil. The statue takes its name from the activity: "The Apoxyomenos" which in English means "he who scrapes", that is scrapes his skin.

"A strigil" from Roman times. The tool essential to athletes in the ancient and Roman world. This particular one was a gift to a deity found in the grave of a man, proving that this person could obviously be distinguished for his athletic prowess.

The olive in Byzantine and modern times

The application and mainly the recording of therapeutic practices based on oil during ancient times contributed to their perpetuation and continuous use during Byzan-

tine years. The religious element and rituals directly linked to the olive and oil increased, thus sustaining the sacred nature they had already acquired in ancient times. Oil production continued uninterrupted mainly to supply Constantinople, where both religious, social and everyday needs were greatly increased. Certain impressive evidence, mainly from travellers, concerning the limited production of oil in Crete, one of the leading

oil-producing areas in Greece, shows that during the 13th and 14th centuries the Venetians did not place much emphasis on oil-producing. Their priority at that time was cultivating vines for producing the renowned wine, malmsey, which became hugely famous beyond the limitations of the island. Later, though, in the 16th century, the development of soap-making became the reason for a return to oil production with the result that by the end of the 17th century, production was focussed on olive oil, with vines and cereals coming second. Crete was now a vast olive-grove exciting the admiration of travellers, such as the Frenchman Pitton de Tourne-

Byzantine lamp decorated with an olive branch in bas-relief.

fort who visited Crete in 1669. During the years of Turkish domination, despite the destruction and pillaging by the conquerors, the production of oil continued. The man however who gave a real boost to oil production in Crete was the governor of Egypt Mohammet Ali who landed on the island in 1822. His legislation included strict measures for the protection of the tree and an increase in production so as to meet the needs of the Egyptian army.

Harvesting olives has remained the same from Byzantine times up to the present day.

POPULAR CUSTOMS & TRADITIONS

Oil, olives, bread and wine make up a traditional meal.

Nutrition

Without doubt the main need the olive and its oil met and continues to meet, that of nutrition with positive effects on healthy physical development, was the reason it became known as sacred, and why it was indissolubly bound to popular traditions, customs and folklore. Initially an essential nutritional element in the areas it flourished, which were almost exclusively agricultural, it came to be part of traditional, time-honoured cooking. In Greek and especially Cretan cuisine, large amounts of oil are consumed, not only because it is readily available but mainly because it beneficial to health. It is a fundamental part not only of daily recipes, but also of those linked to special days, religious festivals, ceremonies and rituals. For example, in religious fasting when the consumption of meat and oil is forbidden, olives are allowed. This is yet another reason why olives are a basic part of Greek and mainly Cretan cooking and are always present in the traditional household. Housewives prepare olives of all kinds: green cracked olives, slit olives, pickled olives, salted olives, etc. which accompany everyday meals. In traditional

22

cooking, olive oil has many different applications. It helps preserve meat, cheese, olives and vegetables. These products are placed in vessels full of oil and sealed. The oil, as in other cases the use of salt, vinegar or brine, ensures their preservation. In the preparation of dough, sacred due to its relation to bread and Artos, oil plays a leading role, needing only to be combined with flour and water to make yet another sacred product. Christianity considers three products sacred: oil, wine and bread. Olive oil is also an essential ingredient in the preparation of pulses, cereals and vegetables. The famous Greek dishes cooked in oil need only oil, water, tomato

Each household's main concern was to safeguard enough oil for the year, which was then stored in large stone jars.

and a few spices to make them healthy and nourishing. Raw olive oil is also greatly consumed, poured over vegetables, salads and fish, or even eaten on its own with bread or rusks. This explains the large consumption of oil in Greece, which amounts to 20 kilos per person per year. In Crete especially the consumption of olive oil is even greater and can reach 27 kilos per person.

The "mistato" was a special jug for measuring oil and held exactly 12.5 kilos.

Oil, the basis of health and beauty

Over the years the olive has never ceased to be regarded as the basis of health, physical well-being, proper development and beauty. These "recipes" have been passed down over the centuries either by practical doctors or by word of mouth, bringing relief and prosperity to those generations who even to the present day have devoutly kept tradition alive and passed it down to their children. Oil is an important part of folklore, which, just as in ancient times, highlights its therapeutic and beautifying properties. These practices obviously flourished mainly in olive-producing areas, such as Crete, the Peloponnese, Central Greece

and Lesbos. It is considered essential for massage in cases of muscular pain, pain in the joints, and rheumatics. One opinion held in the past and still existing today is that in order for a new-born baby's bones and muscles to develop properly, it must be rubbed soon after birth with oil boiled together with sage leaves (wild herb from Crete). The new-born's head should also be rubbed with oil during the first few days of life to prevent or cure common skin problems. Drinking raw olive oil is even today considered extremely beneficial for people with gall bladder problems, stomach ulcers, or constipation. Apart from the oil, the olives themselves are considered therapeutic at the various stages

of ripening. Thus a drop of warm black olive is beneficial in severe earache and crushed green olives are believed to be good for adenopathy. Apart from the healing properties of oil, as already mentioned, its positive results on beauty have been noted from ancient times. Over the centuries it has been constantly used as a basis for cosmetics related to healthy hair. Olive oil is even considered beneficial for the hair of the elderly, when fingertip massage to the hair roots with olive oil is recommended. Hair loss can also be prevented in this way, while at the same time the hair takes on a healthy shine. It is often combined with other herbal extracts for the best possible results. Thus, for shiny black hair, the oil is combined with walnut leaves or root, which leave it manageable, sleek and healthy. Oil is also considered a base for ointments for dry or dehydrated skin.

Lighting - Heating

Olive trees and oil have from ancient times been linked to heating and light. Fires were lit with olive wood and oil ensured light for night work. Lamps burned oil and had one or more wicks depending on the amount of light needed. Oil therefore ensured light thus making night work possible, as well as strengthening family and social ties when after nightfall and the working day was over, family members would gather round the table with the lamp to talk, tell stories or simply relax. Apart from the wood and the oil, during the 1950's the olive pits remaining after pressing began to be used,

and produced a useful fuel. Finally, the use of olive oil for lighting took on a symbolic nature and was used in Christianity in the form of a small hanging oil-lamp burning in front of icons both in churches or homes. One custom says that the first oil produced should be used to light the lamp to thank God for blessing the crop and giving the farmers the strength and health to complete the harvest of this blessed fruit.

Olive oil in soap producing

In ancient times, many ancient civilisations, such as the Phoenicians, the Sumerians, the Egyptians, etc. had discovered and implemented a cleaning product based on oil or fat and ash. In Greece, the preparation of this product was initially based on oil and in the 17th century, the first soap factories appeared, which in the 18th and 19th centuries increased in number and became for many regions, such as Crete, one of the basic resource sectors. It is worth noting that Cretan soap factories exported soap to many European countries, including France, Southern Italy, Malta, etc. Apart from organised soap factories, soap was produced in homes from the residue of the family's oil. Housewives produced their own soap to meet the needs of the household for washing clothes and other equipment. The traditional recipe for soap included olive oil, water and potash in specific proportions. The preparation of home-made soap was a process passed down from one generation to another, an integral part of tradition and particularly of the customs related to everyday life and the home which each mother was obliged to pass on to her daughter, thus equipping her with the knowledge she would one day need to set up her own home.

Home-made soap with olive oil (Old recipe)

Ingredients
3 okas olive oil*
1 oka potassium carbonate
2 okas water

Preparation
Mix the potassium carbonate and water in a large pot and place it the stove. When the mix is warm, and before it boils, slowly add the olive oil to prevent frothing and stir constantly with a wooden ladle. When the mix starts to become thick and rather creamy, the soap is separated and rises to the surface leaving water at the bottom of the pot. Remove the pot from the stove and separate soap from water using a strainer or colander. Place it immediately in mould and, when it thickens, separate it into bars and let it dry.

*1 OKA = 1280gr

THE OLIVE & OLIVE OIL SACRED SYMBOLS

Beyond the practical properties of oil as described in myths, historical evidence and folklore, oil acquired a sacred nature due mainly to the aforementioned beneficial properties regarding its practical use. In Minoan times, as seen from illustrations of the period, both oil and the olive held an extremely important position and were rarely absent from idolatrous rituals, mainly due to the importance of these specific products to nutrition and the economy. Even the olive tree itself, age-old yet continuously regenerating and productive, evoked awe and admiration and thus could only be considered sacred. The ancient Greek world never ceased to regard the tree as sacred due to its link with the goddess Athena, and temples were often surrounded by olive groves. The ancient Greeks anointed their bodies with oil to ensure protection from the gods. It was also used in libations to express their gratitude and beg favour from the gods. Oil also played a leading role in burial customs. Apart from anointing the dead with oil, lamps were filled and placed in the grave as gifts to

The roadside shrines often found in Crete always contain an oil-lamp that must be kept burning as a symbol of the immortal soul of the person lost at that particular place.

According to religious tradition, the lamp must be kept burning before the icon of the Virgin Mary. The oil in the lamp is considered sacred and therapeutic and in Crete it is often rubbed on patients while the sign of the cross is made. Mothers also make the sign of the cross over their children at night, having first dipped their fingers in the oil-lamp. Oil-lamps in homes and churches are always filled with the first oil produced by the farmers to give thanks to God for the good crop.

the gods, to ensure light in the life after death. Offerings to the dead often included olives, while another custom was to place the dead on leaves from the sacred tree. The link between the olive tree and death arises from its shape and features: age-old, evergreen, an old, almost dehydrated trunk from which new life springs in fresh green shoots. In other words, the olive tree symbolises and continues to symbolise a belief in life after death: that death is not an end but a beginning,

the hope for resurrection, rebirth and eternal life. The link between the olive, rebirth and resurrection continued into the years of Christianity, during which olive branches and leaves always accompanied the dead. Olive trees are often planted near graves as a symbol of eternal life and the immortality of the soul, symbolised by the light burning with the oil from the same tree. Even today, traditions and customs surrounding funerals remain intact: the dead body is anointed with oil and wine, olive branches are placed in the coffin along with the oil from the lamp, and finally an oil lamp is lit on the grave and must be kept burning. Generally in Orthodoxy, the sacredness of oil is linked without doubt to the fact that the eternal and divine light is kept burning through the flame in the lamp. Moreover, the chrism, which is the basis of the sacrament of unction, is composed mainly of olive oil combined with other aromatic oils. It is made during Holy Week in a ceremony which culminates on Holy Wednesday when the faithful flock to church to be anointed. Chrism is always to be found in the sanctum in churches and is kept in a special vessel known as a chrismatory.

The ceremony of anointment with chrism is one of the basic parts of the sacrament of unction, baptism that is, which marks man's entry into Orthodoxy. The newly baptised person receives God's blessing and the charisma of the Holy Spirit.

OLIVE OIL
THE SECRET
OF LIFE

The importance of oil in Greek myths and traditions shows its undoubted significance and necessity in daily nutrition. Since ancient times its constituents and chemical composition have been known to form the basis of good health, and this has lead to both the olive tree and its fruit becoming a symbol of worship, prosperity, well-being, purity and sanctification.

In the past as well as today, man's need for a return to natural foods has meant that oil has come to be considered a source of good and healthy living and is included among the 10 most beneficial foods. This was proved beyond a shadow of doubt by the well-known study carried out in seven countries during the 1950's and 60's, concerning epidemiological comparisons between seven areas (Crete, the United States, Japan, Lower Italy, Dalmatia, Corfu and Holland). The comparisons revealed that in Mediterranean areas there is a lower mortality rate and that cases of cancer are much fewer. This amazing difference was put down to dietary habits based mainly on the consumption of olive oil, vegetables, fruit, pulses and cereals, and since then the Mediterranean diet has become a model for good nutrition. The Mediterranean diet differs from the rest in that it includes a greater consumption of oil and consequently, the secret must lie in the constituents of olive oil and mainly in the oleic acid which is a monosaturated fatty acid reaching a proportion of 83%. Apart from the fatty substances, which also include linoleic and linolenic acid, oil contains vitamin E (3-30mg), provitamin A (carotene), minerals, etc. which as anti-oxidants help to protect cells from harm and consequently protect them from various diseases including cancer. According to recent studies, women who consume oil reduce to 25% the chances of contracting breast or ovarian cancer. This explains the lower rate of cases in the Mediterranean in comparison to countries producing less oil. The same applies to cancer of the stomach, prostate and large intestine, which are all linked to dietary habits.

Apart from cancer, oil helps to prevent heart disease. This explains yet again why the Mediterranean peoples who combine the consumption of oil with other dietary habits including dairy products, fruit, vegetables and pulses, have managed to protect themselves from heart disease to a greater extent than other nations. Particularly in Crete it has been medically proven that the mortality rate from coronary heart disease is greatly reduced due to the consumption of olive oil. Oil is of particular benefit to the gastrointestinal tract as it is easily absorbed while at the same time it reduces gastric juices and the creation of satiety. The anti-oxidant substances and in particular vitamins C and E prevent stomach cancer. It has been proved to be of benefit to people suffering from ulcers not only as it eases the pain but also as it often helps the ulcer to heal. Due to the vitamin E and provitamin A, oil helps to protect the skin, not only from solar radiation but also from other skin conditions. It also makes a positive contribution to the normal development and protection of the central nervous system, the brain and the skeleton, and consequently its consumption is considered essential mainly during childhood and the later years, so as to ensure not only correct physical development, but also a healthy old age.

There is no doubt therefore that the secret of good health and longevity lie to a great extent in dietary habits. The Mediterranean diet has been proved to be of great benefit to this end. The consumption of pure, natural products, in the form the earth produces them, ensures the normal and healthy development of the body. Particularly in Crete, the tried and tested "Cretan Diet" constitutes the basis of longevity. To quote the words of the Frenchman Professor Serge Renaud "after fifteen years of study, it has been shown that Crete has the lowest mortality rate…". Other researchers, including the leading dietician Ancel Keys, have been impressed by the liberal even excessive consumption of olive oil in Crete, yet it did not take long for them to realise that this is the basis for health on the island. More specifically, statistics on mortality in industrial countries are impressive if one considers that deaths from coronary heart disease in Crete are 7 : 1 000,000, while in general the mortality rate regardless of reason is 564 : 100,000. This means that Crete has the lowest mortality rate not only in relation to the 7 countries in the study, but world-wide. There is no doubt that the secret of the Cretan's longevity lies in their diet which has remained stable and unchanged since ancient times. It is based on the consumption of olive oil, pulses, fruit, vegetables, cheese, fish, and wine and to a less extent, meat.

	SURVEY IN 7 COUNTRIES		WORLD HEALTH ORGANISATION	
	Coronary Disease	Mortality	Coronary Disease	Mortality
Finland	466	1390	386	1210
US	424	961	263	1061
Netherlands	317	1134	224	1016
Italy	200	1092	148	1066
Yugoslavia	145	1021	137	1302
Corfu	149	847	123	932
Japan	61	1200	53	837
Crete	9	627	7	564

Mortality rate due to coronary heart disease and general mortality (per 100,000 inhabitants) (Serge Renaud: The Mediterranean Diet).

	Coronary Disease	Cancer	Mortality
Finland	972	613	2169
US	773	384	1575
Netherlands	636	781	11825
Italy	462	622	1874
Yugoslavia	242	394	1712
Corfu	202	338	1317
Japan	136	623	1766
Crete	38	17	855

*Mortality rate from the **"Seven country study"** (per 1,000 inhabitants) (Serge Renaud: The Mediterranean Diet).*

FROM THE FRUIT TO THE OIL

The tree and the fruit

It is not only the reputation of Mediterranean oil but also the frequency with which one comes across the olive tree in the particular area, that shows that the olive tree needs sun and light rainfall to flourish. The development and production of quality fruit depend to a great extent on the Mediterranean climate. The olive tree, cultivated in the right environment, is an evergreen, fruit-bearing, long-living tree. Its leaves are grey-green in colour and its trunk over the years may grow to a huge size. It may live for several centuries and, apart from the size, the trunk becomes marked with cavities and lines, very similar to the wrinkles on a human face. Fruit-bearing begins after the first five years of life, that is why it is thought that whoever grows olive trees, apart from his patient nature, is manifesting a need to leave an inheritance to the next generations. The need for patience is also proved by the fact that the olive tree usually only bears fruit every other year. Naturally, according to climate, needs, and technological specifications, the same varieties are not culti-

37

vated in all areas. There are varieties destined for oil production, others for the production of edible olives, as well as those producing "heavy" oil and others "lighter" oil, according to where they are to be used. Some of the main varieties of olive are as follows:

Agrilies: a wild olive tree that takes root by itself and thrives in the same places as the cultivated tree. It may become a tree but we usually come across it as a bush with green leaves and small oval fruit from which low quality oil is extracted.

Koroneiki: also called psilolia due to its small fruit and grown mainly in Crete, the Ionian Islands, the Cyclades, Samos, the Peloponnese and Aitolokarnania. The tree reaches a height of 6-7 metres and the leaves are dark green in colour. The fruit is very small but with a large oil content reaching 27%. The Koroneiki olive produces perhaps the best quality table oil.

Koutsourelies: also called ladolies and is mainly grown in the Peloponnese and Aitolokarnania. The tree, which reaches a height of 7 metres, has dark green leaves and an almost cylindrical fruit with an oil content of 25%, but which is not particularly good quality.

Ladolies from Corfu: grown in Corfu, Paxos and the Ionian Islands. A large tree growing up to 13 metres, which produces leaf-shaped, slightly curved fruit with an oil content reaching 20%. The oil produced from Corfiot olives is of excellent quality and suitable for the table.

Tsunati: also called "mastoid", it thrives in Rethymno and Hania in Crete, Lakonia and Messinia. The tree can reach a height of 8-9 metres, with light green leaves and elongated fruit ending in a nipple. Oil content reaches 20% and it produces fine olive oil.

Mourtolies: this tree which grows in Lakonia can resist cold and drought, reaches a height of 10 metres and has light green leaves. The fruit has a high oil content (24%) which is of very good quality.

Agouromanakolies: grown in Korinthia, Arkadia, Argolida, and is a variety which stands up well to the cold. The tree reaches a height of 7 metres and the oval fruit has a high oil content (30%) which produces an excellent quality table oil.

Adramittini: grown mainly in Lesbos. The tree reaches a height of 8 metres, has dark green leaves and elongated fruit with an oil content of 24%, which produces very good quality oil.

Dafnelies: grows mainly in Samos, Hios and the Cyclades, and the tree reaches a height of 14 metres. The leaves are grey-green and the fruit elongated with an oil content of about 20%.

Throumbes: also called hondroelies, it thrives in Crete, as well as in Samos, Hios, the Cyclades, Rhodes and Attica. The tree is tall reaching up to 10 metres, while the leaves are grey-green. The fruit is elongated and has a high oil content, which can reach 29-30%. Apart from producing oil which can be from good table oil to heavy oil, and according to the time of gathering, the degree of maturity, and the storage time, throumbes can undergo a relatively easy process making them into edible olives of excellent taste and quality. The process includes gathering the fruit, washing and drying it in the sun, and placing it in jars with salt. When the olives are ready, they can be kept in oil.

Valanolies: the most widely spread variety of olive tree in Lesbos, reaching a height of 8 metres. The name comes from the fruit being shaped like an acorn (valanos), and has a high oil content reaching 25%. It is considered one of the best varieties of olives for producing oil.

Vasilikada: thrives mainly in Corfu, Evia, and Halkidiki. A moderately tall tree reaching a height of 8 metres, with green leaves and oval fruit used mainly to produces green edible olives.

Kalamon: grown mainly in Messinia, Lakonia, and Aitolokarnania, and generally in areas with high rainfall. The tree reaches a height of 10 metres and produces elongated, curved fruit. Its oil content is not particularly high (about 17%), but it produces high quality edible olives. The famous Kalamon olives are slit twice lengthwise, placed in water to soak out the bitterness, and then in vinegar. They are kept in pure olive oil.

Korolies: mainly found in Lesbos, Corfu and Zakinthos. A tree 8-10 metres in height, with green leaves and elongated fruit with a relatively low oil content of up to 17%. Mainly used for producing edible olives.

Kolibades: also called milolies, they thrive mainly in the Cyclades, Attica and Messinia. The tree is not particularly tall, possibly reaching a height of 6 metres. The characteristic spherical fruit has a low oil content (about 19%) but produces high quality green, cracked table olives.

Karydolies: thrives in Halkidiki, as well as in Attica, Fthiotida and Evia, reaching a height of 5-8 metres with light, green leaves. The fruit with its characteristic corners has a low oil content (about 15%) but is used to produce high quality black and green edible olives.

Harvesting the fruit

Apart from variety, climate, ground composition and other factors undoubtedly affecting the quality of the olive oil, another crucial factor is the timing of the harvest. Over the years, various theories have been put forward as to when olives should be collected. Some believe that olives should be collected when they are ripe, and others when they are a little under ripe. Whichever theory is implemented however, different things will be achieved. It is certain that very ripe olives produce more oil. Excellence of quality however is ensured when olives are in the first stage of maturity, that is, shortly before they blacken completely. According to recent opinion, the fruit at that stage of maturity produces not only the best but also the most oil, as it is considered that at that particular moment in time, the olive contains the greatest amount of juice. When the fruit is ripe, it is time for the fruit to be harvested, and this is carried out in a number of different ways according to the variety of olive. Hontroelies and throumbes are collected from the ground where they have fallen, either

spontaneously or by thrashing the tree. Hontroelies are usually left to fall spontaneously, which means that they are completely ripe. This is the reason why "thicker" oil is produced from this variety of olive. If of course they are thrashed down at the stage of maturity described above and quickly collected from the ground, then this variety also produces oil of excellent quality. However, the most common method of harvesting used in Crete and other parts of Greece, is that of collecting then from the ground where they have been left to fall naturally. In olden times, the olives were collected straight from the ground by hand. Today the procedure is as follows. At the beginning of winter, before the olives ripen, plastic nets are laid beneath the trees and weighted down with stones. When the olives ripen, or before they fully ripen and the wind

blows, they fall onto the nets. Then the nets are lifted, the olives collected in piles, put into sacks and transported to the olive-press. The nets are left in position all winter, as this procedure, according to the year's production, is repeated several times, each time, that is, that there are enough olives on the nets. It is very important that the olives do not remain for long periods on the nets, as both rainfall and worms favour the growth of fungus and this results in low quality olive oil.

Over recent years, however, apart from olives being allowed to fall spontaneously, the procedure of thrashing is commonly used, in order to achieve the best possible quality of oil. This method ensures the fruit is harvested at the ideal moment of maturity and prevents it being left on the ground where it deteriorates. It requires a net being placed on the cleared ground

beneath the tree, and the branches are thrashed with a wooden pole causing the olives to fall. This pole, which must be curved at one end, has today been replaced by a mechanical one, which not only makes things easier for the producer, but also protects the tree from careless thrusts. Yet there is no doubt that thrashing in one way or another, either with a pole or a mechanical device, damages the fruit, which fall violently to the ground or onto stones and the tree itself may also be damaged. However olives collected in this way produce better quality oil than those collected after falling spontaneously.

Finally, yet another method of collecting olives is "raking". This is mainly used on trees of low height with small fruit, and consists of a kind of rake being dragged through the branches. This method can also damage the fruit and the tree itself, yet it ensures harvesting at the correct moment of maturity.

Crushing the fruit and producing oil

The stage after harvesting consists of separating the fruit from the leaves and dead branches. This is done by "winnowing", during which the collected olives are shaken and the wind blows the leaves away. This is essential as if the leaves remain with the olives, they spoil the taste of the oil. The olives are then placed in special sacks, not plastic ones, but ones that allow the air to circulate, before being transported to the olive-press. The sooner the olives are transported to the press, the better the quality of oil.

Following harvesting, cleaning and transportation, it is time for the fruit to be crushed to extract the oil, a procedure that also plays an important part in its quality. In ancient times, according to accounts by Isiodus, the fruit was crushed in a mortar. Various stages followed during which the pulp was pounded even further, and thus the first distilled natural olive oil was produced. The oil from the pits, naturally of lower quality than the former, was extracted by heating and reheating them for many hours. The technique of pounding and pressing the olives with improvised and manual devices to extract the oil continued for many centuries, even into the Middle Ages and beyond. Only at the beginning of the 20th century did the first oil-presses begin to appear, which of course were

Oil-press at Argyroupoli in Rethymno, as captured by the lens of the traveller, Spratt. "Travels and Researches in Crete" by Captain T.A.B. Spratt, London 1865"

Print by J. Stradanus "Oleum Oli-varum", 16th century, Paris, National Library.

still operated manually and consisted of a cylindrical stone turned by hand with a lever. Later the pressing technique came to be based on cylindrical stones revolving around a central axis, operated either by hand or with the help of animals or even water or steam power.

Today olives are crushed in modern centrifugal presses, in which metal blades crush the fruit and turn them into olive pulp. The pulp is softened and heated simultane-ously in special machines, which helps in the extraction of the oil. Centrifugation follows during which water is added to the pulp and subsequently on the basis of the difference in the specific weight of the contents, the pulp is separated from the oil and the water.

After extraction, the oil is stored either in metallic, rust-proof containers or in glass bottles which are kept in cool storerooms. Up to twenty years ago, the oil was still stored exactly as in ancient times, in earthenware jars, which were kept in store-rooms in the home. Their contents had to be consumed within a year as oil, however good its quality and its storage conditions, does not keep for a great length of time.

QUALITIES OF OLIVE OIL

The quality of olive oil depends on the following characteristics: acidity, oxidation, colour, aroma and flavour. Acidity expresses the percentage of fatty acids in the oil and the greater it is, the thicker and heavier the oil is. The degree of acidity is determined by various factors, such as the time the olives are harvested, the length of time they are left in the sacks, the method of pressing used, and of course whether or not they are diseased. The longer the olives remain on the ground or in the sacks, the more pungent the taste of the oil produced. For this reason cultivators today try to collect the olives as quickly as possible, not to tie them up tightly in sacks, and to take them to the press within two days at the latest. Oxidation depends on the way the oil is stored, which if not suitable, gives the oil an earthy taste. The aroma and flavour of the oil depend mainly on the area, weather conditions, the variety of tree

1915, Panama International Exhibition. Bronze medal and prize awarded to Emmanuel Kaounis, oil producer from Rethymno, Crete, for export of olive oil.

and the time of harvesting. If the fruit is collected early, relatively unripe, the oil produced has a bitter taste. Finally, the colour of the oil, which varies from green to gold and brown, depends mainly on the harvesting time, but also on other factors such as the extraction process.

On the basis of the above criteria, the category of the olive oil is determined according to quality, and are as follows: virgin olive oil, refined olive oil and pure olive oil.

Virgin olive oil is produced from olives that have not been spoilt or processed in any way during pressing. According to acidity levels, it can be separated into the following categories: extra virgin olive oil with an acidity level up to 1%; fine virgin olive oil with an acidity level up to 1.5%; virgin olive oil semi-fine with an acidity level up to 3.3%; and industrial or virgin olive oil lampante with an acidity level high enough to need chemical processing.

Refined olive oil is produced from virgin olive oil lampante. Processing reduces the acidity of industrial oil and produces a thin oil without flavour, and light yellow in colour.

Pure olive oil is a blend of refined and virgin olive oil. It has a light, greenish yellow colour and an acidity level not exceeding 1.5%. The use of the oil is determined according to which category it belongs. Extra virgin olive oil

cane be consumed raw and is the most suitable for salads, greens, vegetables, pulses, etc. Fine virgin olive oil is suitable for cooking or frying, while refined oil is used mainly in confectionery, and particularly in pastry sweets.

At this point a reference must be made to **organic oil**, which is produced from organically cultivated trees, and the juice is extracted using only traditional methods. The production of organic olive oil began in recent years, meeting the need for a return to a natural life and healthy natural products. The production of organic olive oil concerns all stages of the procedure, from cultivating the trees to the actual production of the oil. Young olive trees are planted in areas which have been fallow for several years, only natural fertilisers are used, traps are used for pests such as the olive fly (Dacus oleae) instead of pesticides, and finally the oil is produced completely naturally without any kind of processing.

Let us now take a look at certain basic criteria and ways of selecting the oil we need. Regardless of the quality of oil we choose, it must be in a container or bottle of not more than 5 litres, on which its name, place of origin and name of producer must be stated. It is preferable not to buy unbottled oil of unknown origin as you may be in for a surprise, unless the supplier has produced it himself and is an acquaintance, friend or relation. A law exists, however which prohibits the sale of unbottled oil by the producer. One of the main criteria is the acidity level which must be low, up to 1% at the most. The oil must also be clear and green or greenish yellow in colour. Pure yellow oil is good only if the colour is due to the variety of tree, which is difficult to detect. If oil is bought off the shelf, it is a good idea to make sure it is in a cool place and

Olive oil label from Crete, 1915.

not exposed to the sun. It must be pointed out that oil which is stored in green or other dark-coloured bottles, can better stand possible exposure to the sun. The quality of the oil is considerably affected by the conditions under which it is kept.

AROMATIC OLIVE OILS

Since Minoan and classical times, aromatic oils have been widely used mainly in therapeutics and perfumery. Information has been obtained from Linear B tablets at Knossos, according to which there were special perfumers who prepared aromatic oils for use in therapeutics, as perfumes and as gifts to the dead and deities. Some aromatic oils were possibly used in cooking, and to improve an oil with an unsatisfactory flavour or aroma. As we learn from Aristotle, even in classical times, oil just as wine, was known to be affected by different smells around it. Taking this into consideration, therefore, the oil was simply aromatised according to where it was to be used. An aromatic plant or spices were added to the oil, which in a few days acquired the particular aroma. By aromatising oil, deterioration in its flavour due to the passage of time was avoided, and in this way its life was ex-

tended. This custom was continued in later years when oregano or olive leaves or pits were added to the oil. The main use of aromatic oil, which continues up to the present day, was therapeutic. Oil boiled with labdanum leaves (Cistus creticus) or sage seeds, was good for massage and muscular pains.

Today aromatic oils are mostly used in cooking to improve the flavour of a particular ingredient. They are not often added to the food itself, but poured on to salads, vegetables, pasta, meat and fish, or served as an appetiser with bread instead of butter. Aromatic oils can be bought ready prepared or easily made according to preference. Products usually used are spices, herbs and citrus fruits, which can be added alone or one can experiment with different combinations. Preparation is simple - a very good quality oil with low acidity, the aromatic ingredient carefully dried, and a clean, dry bottle. The ingredients are put in the bottle, which is tightly closed and stored in a dark, cool place. The oil is ready to use in a few days. Below are some ideas for preparing aromatic olive oil:

Olive oil with rosemary

Add a sprig of rosemary and 2-3 peppercorns to a bottle of olive oil. If a more pungent flavour is required, 1-2 cloves of garlic can be added. Close the bottle tightly and store in a cool, dark place for a few days. When ready, remove the herbs.

Olive oil with red peppers

To prepare this wonderful spicy oil which goes well with roast meat and vegetables, simply add 2 dried hot red peppers to a bottle or jar of oil and store in a shady place for two weeks. The same result will be achieved by adding fresh hot red peppers, instead of dried ones.

Olive oil with basil

Add 2-3 sprigs of basil or 1 teaspoon of finely chopped fresh basil to a bottle of oil, close tightly and store for about 10 days in a cool, dark place. This oil goes well with fresh tomatoes and pasta, and if a stronger flavour is required, 2 crushed cloves of garlic and a little pepper can be added.

Olive oil with lemon

Add the rind of a lemon to a small bottle of oil. A teaspoonful of crushed pepper can be added if desired. Close the bottle tightly and store in a cool, dark place for 15-20 days. When the oil is ready, remove the lemon rind. It can be enjoyed on wild greens, salads and even roast meat or fish. Oil with orange or citron can be prepared in the same way and can also be used in confectionery.

Olive oil with oregano

Add a few sprigs of oregano to a bottle of oil, close tightly and keep in a dark place. It is ready in a few days and can be used in many ways, such as on salads, fish, and roast meat

Olive oil with cinnamon and cloves

This oil can be used in confectionery and is easily prepared. Simply add 1-2 cinnamon sticks and 5-6 whole or crushed cloves to a bottle of oil. In about ten days the oil is ready for use.

EDIBLE OLIVES

Olives have become extremely popular due to their abundance in Crete and other olive-producing areas of Greece and to the development of various processes that allow them to be stored for long periods of time and to be prepared to suit all tastes. The olive is an essential part of every Cretan and more generally Mediterranean meal. Large quantities are consumed and most households prepare enough olives to meet their needs for the whole year. The olive can accompany any kind of food and in Crete at least it is considered essential to round off a tasty meal. Although today the popularity of the olive has made it essential at every meal, olive consumption in the past was a result of financial and practical situations. When hardship and poverty did not allow for "luxuries" at daily meals, a few olives and a little bread were enough to feed whole families. Apart from this, however, there were practical reasons for its consumption. Housewives in Crete did not usually spend much time in the home, but worked alongside the men in the fields, cultivating crops and tending the animals. So olives, of which there were plenty, and bread were the basic foods awaiting the family on their return home at night. The close bonds between the olive and our dietary habits are proved by the fact that during periods of fasting in the Orthodox Church, oil is forbidden but olives are allowed. This explains why monasteries are often surrounded by vast olive-groves. One of the basic concerns of the monastery and each monk, was to safeguard the year's supply of olives. Travellers in the 15th and 16th centuries who visited Mount Athos were impressed by the monks' daily food which always included salted olives. The quality of olives and particularly of those destined for the table, is affected by various factors, such as climate, soil, the weather conditions in which they ripened, the method of cultivation, and certainly the method of harvesting. It is known for sure that good quality olives depend on lime, potassium and phosphorus-rich soil, so as to avoid the use of fertilisers which have a negative effect on their taste. Weather conditions at the time the fruit was ripening also play an important part in the quality of the olives. For example, drought causes the fruit to wrinkle making the olives unsuitable for the table. The time and place of harvesting is also crucial to quality. Green table olives are usually harvested from the first ten days in September up to the middle of November. This time span can however change, as the olives ripen according to cultivation, weather conditions and size of crop. Regardless of when the olives do finally ripen, it is crucial that they are closely observed so the fruit is harvested at exactly the right moment, as a premature or delayed harvest can reduce the quality of edible olives. Green table olives must be collected as soon as they take on a greenish yellow colour, have a smooth, shiny skin and are so hard that juice comes out when pressed. Black olives are collected later than green ones, that is, from the middle of October and throughout the winter. Good quality black table olives must have a dark-coloured skin and flesh almost to the pit. They must not be over-ripe as they then become soft and therefore lower quality. Apart from the harvesting time, an important

factor in the quality of edible olives is also the method used, which must not damage the fruit. The most suitable, although not the most profitable way of harvesting is by hand, which avoids damage to the fruit and buds and allows for gradual selection. This procedure though, is more expensive, so usually thrashing is preferred. Nets are spread beneath the tree and a pole or a mechanised device is used to knock the fruit to the ground. The workers must be very careful not to damage the fruit as it is destined for the table. When harvesting is over, the fruit is collected and transported to the place where the edible olives are to be prepared.

Even today, olives are prepared in the same way our forefathers used. Olives have been eaten since ancient times and the method or preparation has remained the same over the years. In Crete, all the varieties are edible regardless of the size of the pit or whether they are fleshy or not. As already mentioned, they fall into two categories: green ones that are harvested almost unripe, and black ones collected when ripe. The most widely spread method of removing their bitter taste is with salt. The only olives not needing this are the so-called

"dates", that is those that ripen on the tree, are washed and are ready to eat. Of course, if they are not eaten immediately, they must be kept in brine or olive oil. Some of the most widely spread methods of preparing edible olives are mentioned below:

Black salted olives (alatsolies)

The fruit is harvested when fairly ripe, washed, left to dry preferably in the sun, and placed in baskets in layers with coarse salt (ratio 1:3) for about one month. It must be stirred every day. When the olives have lost their bitter taste and their water, they are stored in earthenware jars.

Black olives in brine

The olives are harvested when ripe, that is, when their flesh is firm and they take on a purplish-black colour. They are washed well and stored in brine in wood or plastic containers. A weight is placed on top of the olives to keep them under the brine, and every so often, salt is added which on the one hand destroys microorganisms, yet on the other hand, can cause the olives to wrinkle if excessive. They must be kept in the brine for 2-6 months, and when they lose their bitter taste, they are preserved in fresh, lighter brine.

Pickled black olives

Smooth, firm olives are harvested as soon as they ripen and take on a purplish-black colour. They are washed well and placed in a container with equal amounts of oil, salt and vinegar in a ratio of 1:15 with the olives (e.g. 15 kilos olives + 1 kilo salt + 1 litre oil + 1 litre vinegar). Fill up with water and in about 10 days they will have lost their bitterness, and can be consumed straight from the container.

Kalamon olives

Black olives of the Kalamon variety are scored twice lengthwise and placed in plain water, which is changed twice a day until they lose their bitterness. In 6-10 days, after verifying that the olives are no longer bitter, they are placed in a container with vinegar for 2-3 days, and then stored in light brine.

Green cut olives

Large, firm, green olives are chosen which are scored lengthwise with a sharp knife or blade, taking care not to reach the pit. To remove bitterness, place in water for 10 days, changing daily. When ready, they can be stored in brine (prepared as for Green Cracked Olives).

Green cracked olives

To prepare cracked olives, they must be collected when still green and hard, that is at the beginning of autumn. They must be cracked with a stone or other tool, taking care not to break the pit, and placed in water for about 10 days to remove bitterness. The water must be changed every day. As soon as they lose their bitterness, they are ready to be eaten. They can be stored in brine prepared as follows: place an unbroken egg in a container of water and add as much salt as needed for the egg to rise to the surface and reveal shell the size of a coin. When this happens, the brine is ready. Remove the egg and put in the olives together with the rind of a lemon.

STORAGE IN OIL

Before freezers came to be used in the kitchen, but mainly before it was discovered how to cultivate and produce all products throughout the year, oil was used for preserving food, to safeguard certain products both in and out of season, and save money by storing them at a time of plenty. Food preservation is a simple procedure requiring the product to be firstly dried, either in the sun or the oven, and then kept in a glass container with oil, vinegar and salt. Pickles, as products preserved in oil are called, provide an excellent way of enriching daily meals with all kinds of food, regardless of season. For example, in summer, various vegetables which are in abundance at that time of year, can be collected, brought to the boil in a pan and, when cold, placed in a clean, dry, glass container full of oil. Pickled vegetables are delicious and can be preserved all winter. Pickled Florina peppers can be preserved in the same way and provide a tasty accompaniment to any meal, regardless of season. The peppers must be well washed, seeds removed, placed in a grill for 10-15 minutes or boiled for 2-3 minutes, then salted and placed in a clean, dry, glass jar full of oil. 2-3 cloves of garlic can be added if desired.

Tomatoes, in abundance during the summer, are another product commonly preserved in oil, to be eaten during the winter. Tomato puree can be made as follows: very ripe tomatoes are used which are washed well, the skins and seeds removed, then they are pulped and strained through a fine sieve or cloth to remove all liquid. They are then spread out in the sun or baked in the oven. When ready, they are placed in a glass container, which is filled with oil and tightly closed. Tomato puree can be preserved for long periods of time. Apart from vegetables, cheeses can also be preserved in oil, to which according to their kind, various spices or aromatic plants can be added to produce different flavours.

THE OLIVE MUSEUM AT KAPSALIANA RETHYMNO CRETE

One of the largest olive-groves not only in Crete but in the Mediterranean as a whole, is located near Rethymno, in the Municipality of the same name and near the historic Monastery of Arkadio. The settlement of Kapsaliana, a dependency of the monastery, lies in the same area, and among its 15 buildings is the monastery oil-mill. Up to 1958, the oil-mill was in operation and the settlement was home to 15 families. In later years, however, it was abandoned and fell into ruins. In 1955, it was declared a settlement of high cultural value, and its owners reconstructed it as a labour of love. Today the completely restored settlement, dating back to the years of Venetian domination, can be visited and admired. The Olive Museum could not have found a better home than the monastery oil-mill, which was most probably built in 1763 by the Reverend Father of Arkadio, Philaretus. This building, together with the neighbouring privately-owned oil-mill, the storeroom, the monk-caretaker's cell and the Cretan dwelling provide the visitor with information on olive and oil production, and the age-old, sacred relationship between Man, the olive and its oil.

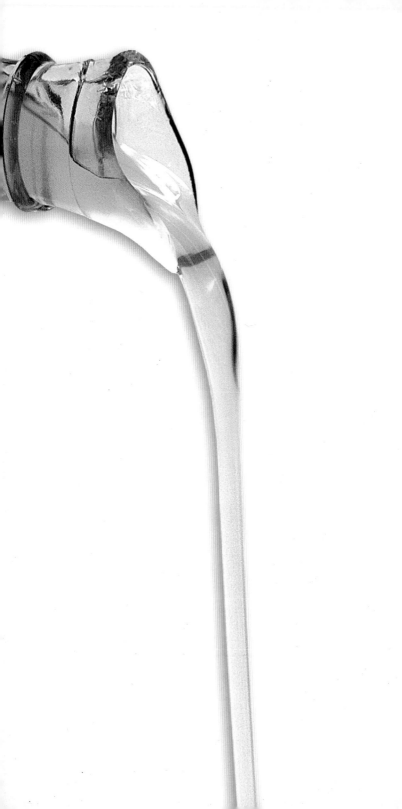

Salads

Artichoke salad

Small artichokes or
large ones cut into 4
Oil
Vinegar
Salt

Wash the artichokes, cut into pieces if large, and put in a bowl of water to prevent from going black. Prepare pickling-brine as follows: put a whole egg in a bowl of water and enough salt for the egg to rise to the surface and float. When this happens, the brine is ready. Put the artichokes into the brine and leave covered for a whole day. The following day, pour off the brine, put the artichokes in a glass bowl and cover with oil. Serve with a little lemon or vinegar.

Country salad

1 tomato
1 cucumber
1 piece of feta cheese
½ onion
Savoury olives
2-3 tablesp. olive oil
Salt

Wash the vegetables well and cut into small pieces. Arrange on a plate with the feta and olives. Sprinkle with salt and oil, and the salad is ready. A little oregano sprinkled on top of the feta adds to the taste.

Wild greens salad

1 kilo wild greens
Salt
Lemon juice
Olive oil

Clean the greens, cut if need be, and wash very carefully. Heat a large pan of water and when it boils, put in the greens. Simmer for 20 minutes. Take off the heat, strain, add salt and serve cold or hot with lemon juice and plenty of olive oil.

Cretan Dakos

1 barley rusk (square)
1 tomato
1 piece of feta cheese
2-3 tablesp. oil
Salt
Onion
Oregano

Wet the rusk and dry with a clean towel. Grate the tomato and feta and spread on the rusk. Add the oil, salt, oregano and if liked, a little grated onion.

Beetroot salad

Beetroot
Oil
Vinegar

Wash the beetroot and boil in plenty of salted water. When soft, drain and cut into rings or into 4 lengthways. Place in a bowl and cover with oil and vinegar.

Bulbs

1 kilo edible bulbs
Oil
Vinegar
Salt
Garlic

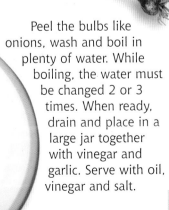

Peel the bulbs like onions, wash and boil in plenty of water. While boiling, the water must be changed 2 or 3 times. When ready, drain and place in a large jar together with vinegar and garlic. Serve with oil, vinegar and salt.

Taramosalata

150 gr. fish roes (taramas)
300 gr. stale bread
4 tablesp. lemon juice
1 glass olive oil
2-3 walnuts

Crumble the bread and place in mixer bowl with the fish roes. Beat, adding alternatively small amounts of oil and lemon juice until the mixture is smooth and creamy. Chopped walnuts can be added, and the salad is served garnished with black olives.

Garlic sauce

6 cloves of garlic
1 cup breadcrumbs
Salt
Juice of one lemon
2 teasp. vinegar
1 cup olive oil

Crush the garlic with pestle and mortar. Add salt and breadcrumbs moistened with water. Gradually add alternatively the oil, lemon juice and vinegar, and beat well until the garlic sauce is as soft as required.

Sauces

Oil and vinegar dressing

1 cup olive oil
½ cup vinegar
Salt

Mix the ingredients well and the oil and vinegar dressing is ready. It makes a delightful accompaniment to salads and boiled vegetables.

Oil and lemon sauce

1 cup oil
4 tablesp. lemon juice
½ teasp. salt

Beat ingredients well together and the oil and lemon sauce is ready. If a spicier flavour is required, add 1 teasp. mustard. Delightful served with grilled fish, vegetables and salads.

Egg and lemon sauce

2 eggs
Juice of one lemon
1-2 cups broth from food

Beat the eggs and gradually add the lemon juice. While continuing beating, gradually add the broth from the food and then pour the sauce back into the pan, stirring constantly.

Mayonnaise

1 litre oil
3/4 cup lemon juice
4 egg yolks
1 teasp. salt

Separate the eggs putting the yolks in a basin together with the salt, and mix well (if mixed by hand, only in one direction). Gradually add the oil and when about half has been added, start adding oil and lemon alternatively. When the mayonnaise thickens, place in a glass container and keep refrigerated. Goes well with fish.

Bechamel sauce

1 kilo milk
8 tablesp. corn flour
3 eggs
Salt - pepper
Nutmeg
1 small cup oil

Heat the milk, first putting a little in a small pan to dissolve the corn flour. Gradually add the dissolved corn flour to the warm milk stirring constantly. Add salt, pepper, nutmeg and the oil and continue to stir until the sauce thickens. Remove from the heat and add the beaten eggs.

Pulses

Bean soup

½ kilo dried beans
½ kilo tomatoes
2 green peppers
2 carrots
2 onions
2 celery roots
Salt - pepper
1 cup olive oil

Soak the beans overnight in water. The following day change the water and boil the beans for about 15 minutes. Change the water again and add the onions, celery, tomatoes and peppers, all finely chopped, salt, pepper and the oil. Simmer for 20 minutes and then add the carrot chopped in rings. Simmer for approximately 1 ½ hours.

Baked butter beans

½ kilo butter beans
1 onion
1-2 cloves of garlic
1 bunch celery leaves
2 tomatoes
1 teasp. sugar
Salt -pepper
1 cup olive oil

Soak the beans overnight in water. The following day, rinse and boil for half an hour. Finely chop the onion, fry in hot oil and add the garlic, celery, tomato, sugar and one cup of water. Simmer the beans in the sauce for about half an hour. Place the beans in a baking dish, cover with the sauce, and season. Bake for about 40 minutes.

Black-eyed peas with fennel

½ kilo black-eyed peas
½ kilo tomatoes
1 bunch of fennel
1 onion
Salt - pepper
1 cup olive oil

Boil the peas in plain water for about half an hour, remove from the heat and drain. Chop the tomatoes, fennel and onion. Heat a little oil and saute the onion and fennel. Add the chopped tomatoes and two cups of water, and simmer for about 20 minutes. Finally add the peas and a little more water if need be. Simmer until cooked.

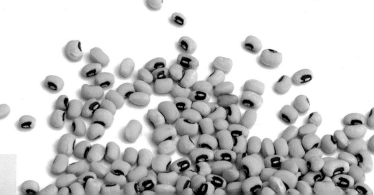

Broad bean puree

½ kilo broad beans
1 onion
1 cup olive oil

Soak the beans in water overnight. The following day, rinse and put on to boil for about half an hour. Remove from heat and drain. When cold, skin the beans and put in a pan with 2 cups of salted water. When they are very soft and have soaked up the water, remove from the heat. Before serving, pour fresh olive oil over the beans and garnish with finely chopped onion.

Lentils

½ kilo lentils
2-3 tomatoes
1 onion
1 bay leaf
Salt -pepper
1 cup olive oil

Wash lentils and put on to boil. After 10 minutes, add the finely chopped onion and tomato, salt, pepper, bay leaf, oil, and one cup of water. Simmer for about an hour.

Lentils with rice

1 cup of lentils
½ cup rice
2 medium onions
Salt
1 cup olive oil

Put the lentils on to boil in plain water. Change the water and when it boils, add the rice and salt and leave to simmer. Saute the finely chopped onion and add to the pan together with the oil. Stir well and when the rice is cooked and the food thickens, turn off the heat.

Vegetables

Stuffed vine leaves (Dolmadakia)

800 gr. rice
300 gr. vine leaves
5 courgettes
2 potatoes
3 round aubergines
2 kilos tomatoes
3 onions
10 courgette flowers
2 cups oil
Mint
Parsley
Dill

Blanch the vine leaves, wash and chop the herbs. Carefully scoop out the centres of the tomatoes, potatoes, aubergines and courgettes with a spoon or potato peeler, and put the tomato pulp and some pulp from the other vegetables in a bowl for the stuffing. Add to this the chopped herbs, grated onion, rice, oil, a little water from the vine leaves and the salt. Arrange the vegetables in a baking dish and fill them with the stuffing mixture. Place a little stuffing on each vine leaf and roll up, taking care not to let the stuffing escape from the sides. Do the same with the courgette flowers. When all are stuffed and the dish full, pour the remaining stuffing over the vegetables, adding a little oil and water. Bake in oven.

Okra in tomato sauce

1 kilo okra
1 cup oil
1 medium onion
2-3 tomatoes
Salt, pepper

Prepare, wash, drain and salt the okra. Heat the oil in the pan and add the onion. Before it browns, add the chopped tomatoes and pepper. Bring to the boil, add the okra, and if necessary, a little water. Simmer for about 30 minutes.

Spinach with rice

1 kilo spinach
1 cup rice
1 onion
1 bunch dill
Salt - pepper
1 cup olive oil

Prepare and wash the vegetables well. Heat the oil in a pan and saute the chopped onion, then add the dill and spinach. Add a cup of water and bring to the boil before adding the rice. Add salt and pepper and leave to simmer. When ready, take off the heat and serve with lemon.

Green beans in tomato sauce

1 kilo fresh green beans
½ kilo tomatoes
1 onion
Salt - pepper
1 cup olive oil

String the beans and wash well. Saute the onion and then add the beans. Add the chopped tomatoes, salt, pepper, and a cup of water and simmer for about 45 minutes. After half an hour, if desired, 2 potatoes cut in cubes can be added, and when the food is cooked, a cup of crumbled feta cheese.

Baked vegetables (Briam)

3 aubergines
4-5 courgettes
4-5 potatoes
½ kilo tomatoes
3 onions
2 green peppers
Chopped parsley
2 cups oil
Salt - pepper

Prepare and wash vegetables well, slice, salt and arrange in a baking dish. Add the oil and a cup of water and bake in the oven for about an hour. If desired, before placing in oven, pieces of feta cheese or trahanas can be added.

Fried aubergines with tomato sauce

1 kilo flask aubergines
4-5 ripe tomatoes
4 cloves of garlic, crushed
Salt - pepper
½ cup olive oil

Wash and slice the aubergines, sprinkle with salt and leave for about half an hour. Rinse, drain well and fry. In another pan, heat the oil, saute the garlic and add the chopped tomatoes. Season, add one cup of water and simmer until the sauce thickens. Arrange the fried aubergines in a baking dish, pour over the tomato sauce and bake in the oven for 15-20 minutes.

Baked aubergines with tomatoes and herbs (Imam bayildi)

3 aubergines
3 tomatoes
1 oniaon
3-4 cloves of garlic
1 soupspoon chopped parsley
1 soupspoon chopped dill
Salt - pepper
1 cup olive oil

Cut the aubergines in half, drain and place in baking tin. Chop tomatoes and onions and mix with dill, parsley, salt, pepper and oil, and spread mixture over the aubergines. Add a cup of water and bake for about half an hour.

Fried aubergines

1 kilo flask aubergines
3-4 tablesp. flour
Salt
Grated cheese
Beer
Olive oil for frying

Prepare the aubergines, slice and dip each one into the beer. Drain well, season and coat in flour. Heat the oil in a frying pan and fry the aubergines. When golden brown, arrange on a serving dish and garnish with grated cheese.

Artichokes with yoghurt

2 kilos artichokes
1 kilo sour yoghurt
1 onion
1 cup oil
1 lemon
1 tablesp. flour
Salt - pepper

Prepare the artichokes and place in a bowl of water with the lemon juice and the flour. Saute the onion in the oil and carefully add the artichokes. Add salt and pepper and half an hour later the yoghurt.

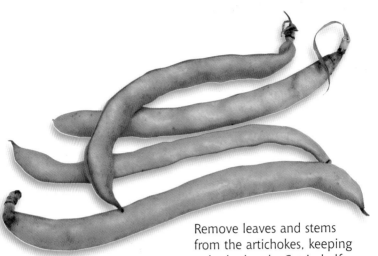

Artichokes with broad beans

8-10 artichokes
1 kilo broad beans
1 bunch dill
1 bunch spring onions
2 lemons
2 tablesp. flour
1 cup olive oil

Remove leaves and stems from the artichokes, keeping only the heads. Cut in half and place in bowl of water with the flour and lemon juice. Pod the beans and set aside with some of the pods. Chop the onions and saute in hot oil, adding the artichokes, beans, dill, salt, pepper and two cups of water. Bring to the boil, adding the other spoonful of flour dissolved in the juice of a lemon. Cook for about an hour on a low heat.

Artichoke omelette

4 eggs
3 artichokes
Salt, pepper
Olive oil for frying

Prepare the artichokes and place in a bowl of water and lemon juice. Next cut them in small pieces and put in frying pan without oil to soften a little. Add the oil and saute. Beat the eggs and add to the pan with the artichokes. Season and turn the omelette to cook both sides.

Courgette omelette (Sfoungato)

2 kilos small courgettes
7 eggs
250 gr. crumbled feta cheese
Olive oil for frying

Wash and slice the courgettes and boil in salted water. Drain and mix with the crumbled cheese. Heat the oil in the frying pan. Beat four eggs, add to pan, stirring constantly so as not to stick. Place a layer of courgettes on top and cover with the rest of the beaten eggs. Season and turn the omelette to cook the other side. It is ready to eat in a few minutes, but can also be enjoyed cold.

Slice the courgettes and potatoes, salt and coat in flour. Spread the pastry sheets in a baking dish and place a layer of courgettes on top, adding crumbled feta cheese, mint and oil. Arrange a layer of potatoes on top, continuing with alternate layers of courgette and potato. Finally pour over the fresh cream and bake in the oven for about 1 ½ hours.

Boureki

1 kilo courgettes
1 kilo potatoes
½ kilo Cretan feta cheese
3 cups oil
A few mint leaves
Fresh cream
Salt - pepper
Pastry sheets (fyllo)

Courgette patties

1 kilo courgettes
1 cup flour
1 cup fine dried bread-crumbs
250 gr. feta cheese
2 eggs
Parsley
Salt - pepper
Olive oil for frying

Prepare the courgettes, grate, salt and leave to drain. Place in a bowl with crumbled feta cheese, breadcrumbs, beaten eggs, parsley and pepper and knead together. Shape patties, flour and fry in hot olive oil.

Wash and chop the tomatoes. Heat the oil in a frying pan, add the tomatoes and seasoning, and simmer until sauce thickens. Next add the grated cheese and the eggs, taking great care not to break the yolks. When the egg whites set, the food is ready. Take off the heat and serve each egg with a little tomato sauce.

Fried eggs with tomato sauce

5 eggs
4-5 ripe tomatoes
250 gr. feta or kefalotiri cheese
Salt - pepper
Olive oil for frying

Egg and tomato omelette (Strapatsada)

1 kilo tomatoes
5 eggs
Salt - pepper
½ cup of feta cheese
½ cup oil

Wash and chop the tomatoes. Beat the eggs and mix with the tomatoes. Season. Heat the oil in the frying pan and add the mixture. Stir well and when cooked, cover with crumbled feta cheese.

Potatoes in tomato sauce

1 kilo small potatoes
3 ripe tomatoes
1 onion
1 clove of garlic
Salt - pepper
½ cup olive oil

Peel and wash the potatoes. If they are small leave whole, if not cut into cubes. Heat the oil in a pan and saute the chopped onion. Add the chopped tomatoes, crushed garlic, potatoes, seasoning and two cups of water, and leave to simmer until the potatoes are soft and the sauce thickens.

Oven-baked potatoes

1 kilo potatoes
Juice of one lemon
Oregano
Salt - pepper
1 cup olive oil

Peel the potatoes, wash and cut into cubes. If the potatoes are very small, leave them whole and simply score with a knife. Place in a baking dish and sprinkle with salt, pepper and oregano. Pour over the oil, lemon juice, and 2 cups of water and stir well. Bake in the oven for about an hour.

Wild greens omelette

½ kilo asparagus or wild greens
5 eggs
250 gr. crumbled feta cheese
Salt - pepper
Olive oil for frying

Prepare and wash the greens well and boil in lightly salted water. Drain well, chop and mix with the crumbled feta. Heat the oil in the frying pan and add half the beaten eggs. When the omelette sets, spread on the greens and then cover with the rest of the eggs. Turn the omelette to cook the other side and it is ready to eat in a few minutes.

Meat & minced meat dishes

Hare with onions (Stifado)

1 hare 2.5 - 3 kilos
3 kilos small pickling onions
2-3 bay leaves
1 bowl finely
chopped tomatoes
2 cloves garlic
A few cloves
1 glass red wine
1 cup olive oil

Wash and cut the hare or rabbit into portions. Peel the onions and stick a clove into a few. Saute the meat in hot oil and add the onions. Cover the pan for a few minutes and then add the glass of red wine. Add the tomato, bay leaves, salt, pepper and 2 cups of water. Simmer for about an hour. Serve with fried potatoes.

Rabbit casserole with pasta

1 rabbit
½ kilo manestra (small pasta the size of rice)
3-4 ripe tomatoes
1 onion
Cinnamon
Salt - pepper
1 cup olive oil

Wash the rabbit and cut into portions. Heat the oil in a pan and saute the onion. Next saute the rabbit turning constantly. Add the tomatoes, salt, pepper and 2 cups of water and bring to the boil. When half cooked, transfer to a baking dish or preferably a clay cooking pot with a lid, add 2 cups of hot water and put it in the oven for 30 - 40 minutes.

Rabbit in wine

1 rabbit
2 glasses red wine
2 onions
1 clove garlic
1 sprig of thyme
1 bay leaf
1 clove
2 tablesp. flour
Salt - pepper
1 cup olive oil

Several hours or even the day before, prepare the marinade by mixing the wine, onions, crushed garlic, bay leaf, thyme and clove, and put in the rabbit, cut in portions. Remove the pieces of rabbit, drain and coat in flour. Heat the oil and carefully fry the rabbit until golden brown. Add the marinade and one glass of water and simmer for about 1 - 1½ hours.

Chicken with pickled olives

1 ½ kilo chicken
4-5 ripe tomatoes
150 gr. black pickled olives
10 small onions
1 clove garlic
1 glass wine
Oregano
1 cup oil

Wash the chicken, cut into portions, season and leave to drain. Heat the oil in a pan and saute the meat with the onions and garlic. Pour on the wine and add the chopped tomatoes, oregano, pepper, a little salt, and 2 cups of water. Simmer for about 45 minutes and then add the stoned olives. Simmer for another 15 minutes.

Chicken in wine

1 chicken
1 onion
2 cloves garlic
1 bowl finely
chopped tomatoes
1 glass red wine
Salt - pepper
1 cup olive oil

Wash the chicken and cut into portions. Saute the chopped onion, garlic and the meat in hot oil. After a few minutes, pour in the wine adding the tomatoes, salt, pepper and 2 cups of water. Simmer for about an hour. Serve with fried potatoes or rice.

Chicken with lemon and potatoes

1 chicken
2 kilos small potatoes
½ cup lemon juice
Oregano
Salt - pepper
1 cup olive oil

Wash and joint the chicken. Saute in hot oil and then add the lemon juice, potatoes, oregano, seasoning and 2 cups of water. Simmer for about 1 hour.

Lamb with okra

1 kilo lamb
1 kilo okra
½ kilos tomatoes
1 onion
Salt - pepper
1 cup olive oil

Wash the okra and trim the tops. Cut the meat into portions and saute in hot oil with the finely chopped onion. Pour the juice from the tomatoes into the pan and bring to the boil. Add the okra, seasoning and 2 cups of water, and leave to simmer.

Lamb with courgettes

1 kilo lamb
1 kilo courgettes
3-4 ripe tomatoes
1 onion
Parsley
2-3 tablesp. flour
Salt - pepper
½ cup olive oil

Wash the meat, cut into portions, season and coat in flour. Saute the finely chopped onion with the meat in hot oil. Add the chopped tomatoes, the finely chopped parsley and 2 cups of water. Put the lid on the pan and simmer for 1 hour. Meanwhile, wash the courgettes, slice or if small, leave whole, and add to the pan with the meat. Simmer for a further half an hour.

Wash the meat and cut into portions. If it is a leg of lamb, do not cut up, simply score so it cooks better. Brush with oil and place in a baking tin. Peel the potatoes, preferably small ones that can be left whole, otherwise, cut into medium-sized pieces and score. Place in the tin with the meat, sprinkle with salt, pepper, thyme, lemon juice and the remaining oil, and roast in a moderate oven for about 2 hours.

Roast lamb with potatoes

1 kilo lamb
½ kilo potatoes
Juice of one lemon
Thyme
Salt - pepper
½ cup olive oil

Lamb fricassee

1 kilo lamb
½ kilo onions
1 kilo parsley or 3 lettuces
2 eggs
1 lemon
Salt - pepper
½ cup oil

Wash the meat, cut into portions and season. Saute the coarsely chopped onions in hot oil, then add the meat. Fry well, then add ½ cup water and leave to simmer. Wash the parsley well and add to the meat in the pan. Season well. When the food is almost ready, beat the eggs, gradually adding the lemon juice and a little broth from the food. Pour the egg mixture into the pan, joggle the pan a little and the food is ready.

Lamb fricassee can be made with lettuce instead of parsley using exactly the same recipe.

Lamb casserole with pasta

1 kilo lamb
½ kilo manestra
(small pasta the size of rice)
½ kilo tomatoes
1 onion
1 garlic
1 cup olive oil

Wash the meat, cut into portions, and place in a casserole. Add the tomatoes, finely chopped onion and garlic, seasoning, oil and 1 cup of water. Place casserole in oven and leave to cook. When the meat is almost tender, add the manestra and leave until ready.

Veal in wine

½ kilo veal
3-4 ripe tomatoes
3 small onions
1 glass red wine
2-3 bay leaves
½ cup olive oil

Cut the meat into cubes. Wash the vegetables and cut into large pieces. Saute first the vegetables in hot oil and then the meat, turning constantly. Add the chopped tomatoes, wine, bay leaves, and seasoning. Transfer to a baking dish or Pyrex and bake in the oven for about 1½ hours.

Veal in tomato sauce

1 kilo veal
1 onion
2 cloves garlic
1 kilo finely chopped tomatoes
1-2 bay leaves
1 cinnamon stick
3-4 cloves
1 glass red wine
Salt - pepper
1 cup olive oil

Wash the veal and cut into portions. Saute the finely chopped onion, garlic and the veal in hot oil. Pour in the wine and add the tomatoes, bay leaf, cloves, cinnamon, salt, pepper and 2 cups of water. Simmer for about an hour. Served with fried potatoes, rice or pasta.

Veal with green peppers

1 kilo veal
4-5 ripe tomatoes
1 kilo green peppers
½ kilo onions
Salt - pepper
1 cup olive oil

Cut the meat into cubes.
Saute the meat in hot oil in a pan and then add the finely chopped onion, the coarsely chopped green peppers and tomatoes, and the seasoning. Saute on all sides and then add 2 cups water. Simmer until the liquid is reduced.

Veal with green olives

1 kilo veal
½ kilo green olives
3-4 ripe tomatoes
1 clove garlic
Cinnamon
Salt - pepper
1 cup olive oil

Wash the meat and cut into small pieces. Saute in hot oil until golden brown. Add the chopped tomatoes, crushed garlic, cinnamon, seasoning and 1 cup of water. Simmer for about 20 minutes. Meanwhile, put the green olives in hot water and when the meat is half cooked, add to the pan. Simmer for another half an hour.

Pork with wild greens (Tsitsirista)

1 kilo pork
½ kilo wild greens
2-3 onions
Salt - pepper
1 cup olive oil

Prepare and wash the greens well. Wash the meat, cut into portions, and saute in hot oil until half cooked. In the meantime, chop the greens and onions and add to the pan with the meat, season, put on the lid, turn the heat low, and leave to cook in the juices from the greens for about an hour.

Pork with celery

1 kilo pork
1 ½ kilo celery
2-3 onions
2 lemons
Salt - pepper
1 cup olive oil

Cut the meat into portions, season and put in the pan with water. When half boiled, add the oil, finely chopped onion, and the celery, washed and cut into 5cm pieces. Simmer for about an hour.

Pork in wine

½ kilo pork
½ cup red wine
Salt - pepper
½ cup olive oil

Wash the meat well and cut into small pieces. Heat the oil and fry the meat. When half cooked, pour in the wine, season, cover the frying pan and leave on a low heat until the sauce is reduced and only the oil is left.

Meatballs in egg and lemon sauce

1 kilo minced veal
1 teacup rice
2 grated onions
3 tablesp. flour
3 egg yolks
1 egg white, beaten into meringue
Juice of 2 lemons
1 bunch parsley, finely chopped
Salt - pepper
1 cup oil

Put the minced meat, grated onion, rice, parsley, and small glass of water in a bowl and mix well, adding the meringue at the end. Shape small balls from the mixture and coat in flour. Pour 2 litres of water into a pan, bring to the boil, add a little salt, oil, and the meatballs and simmer for about 1½ hours. When ready, beat the egg yolks, gradually adding the lemon juice and a little broth from the pan. Pour the egg and lemon mixture into the pan, remove from the heat and serve immediately.

Meatballs with garlic (Soutzoukakia)

½ kilo minced meat
2 slices bread
4-5 ripe tomatoes
2 cloves garlic
1 egg
½ cup red wine
½ teasp. cumin
Salt - pepper
½ cup oil

Knead the minced meat in a bowl with the breadcrumbs soaked in wine, crushed garlic, egg, salt, pepper and cumin. Shape the mixture into round or sausage-like rolls and leave for about an hour for the flavours to mingle. Heat the oil in a pan and lightly fry the meatballs. Add the chopped tomatoes, 1 cup of water, a little salt, and as soon as the sauce starts to thicken, transfer the meatballs and sauce to a baking dish and bake in the oven for about half an hour.

Moussaka

700 gr. minced meat
2 large aubergines
1 kilo potatoes
4-5 courgettes
2 tomatoes
1 onion
Parsley
Salt - pepper
½ cup oil and oil for frying
Bechamel sauce (see sauces)

Slice the vegetables and fry each kind separately. Heat more oil and saute the onion with the minced meat, adding the chopped tomatoes, parsley, and seasoning, and simmer for about 20 minutes. Arrange a layer of fried potatoes on the bottom of a baking dish, a layer of courgettes on top of this, and then the minced meat and the aubergines. Finally pour over the bechamel sauce and place the dish in a pre-heated oven for about 45 minutes.

Stuffed aubergines (papoutsakia)

½ kilo minced veal
11 long aubergines
2 grated onions
1 bunch parsley, finely chopped
3 chopped tomatoes
Cinnamon
Salt - pepper
1 cup oil

Wash the aubergines, slit lengthwise and scoop out the pulp with a teaspoon, so they resemble boats. It is preferable to leave on the stems. Fry lightly and leave to drain while preparing the meat. Heat ½ cup of oil in a pan and saute grated onion. Add the minced meat, stirring constantly, and then the tomatoes, parsley, cinnamon, seasoning, and simmer for about ½ an hour. Arrange the aubergines in a baking dish, fill each with the meat mixture, and pour over bechamel sauce if desired. Bake for about ½ an hour.

Snails in tomato sauce

1 kilo large snails
4-5 tomatoes
½ kilo onions
½ garlic
½ cup vinegar
1 sprig rosemary
Salt - pepper
1½ cups olive oil

Place the snails in a bowl of water to soften the outside and then scrape clean the shells. Rinse well and leave to drain. Heat the oil in a pan and saute the onions and garlic. Add the tomatoes, vinegar, rosemary, salt, pepper and 1 cup of water. Simmer for about 10 minutes before adding the snails. Cook for a further hour.

Fried snails

½ kilo snails
1 cup vinegar
1 sprig rosemary
Salt
½ cup oil

Place the snails in a bowl of water to soften the outside and then scrape the shells clean. Put the frying pan on the heat and cover the bottom with salt. Place the snails on the salt shells upwards, and leave for a while. Pour on the oil, and a few minutes later, add the vinegar and rosemary. Cover the frying pan, bring to the boil, remove from the heat and the dish is ready.

Fish-Seafood

Octopus with pasta

1 kilo octopus
½ kilo pasta (tubetti)
3-4 ripe tomatoes
1 large onion
½ cup red wine
Salt - pepper
1 cup olive oil

Soak the octopus overnight to soften. If already soft, cut into pieces, wash and drain. Heat the oil in a pan and saute the chopped onion. Add the octopus, stir and pour in the wine. Add the water and allow to simmer on a low heat. When half cooked, add the chopped tomatoes, salt, pepper, and cook well. Remove from pan with a skimmer and cook the pasta in the remaining sauce. Serve the octopus with the hot pasta.

Cuttlefish with fennel

1 kilo cuttlefish
1 kilo fennel
2 spring onions
1 tablesp. flour
1 lemon
Salt - pepper
1 cup olive oil

Prepare, wash and boil the cuttlefish. When soft, remove from the heat and cut into pieces. Cut and boil the fennel. Put the oil, fennel, chopped onions, cuttlefish, and seasoning in a pan. Cook for about half an hour and when ready, add the flour dissolved in the lemon juice to thicken the sauce.

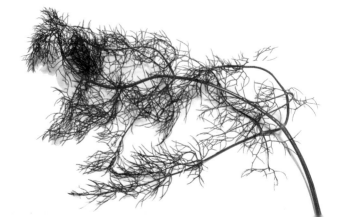

Oven-baked anchovies

1 kilo fresh anchovies
2 lemons
1 teasp. oregano
Salt - pepper
½ cup olive oil

Clean the anchovies, discard the heads and wash well. Place in a baking dish, sprinkle with oregano, lemon juice, oil and a little water, season, and bake in the oven for about 40 minutes.

Fried squid

1 kilo squid
Flour
2 lemons
Salt
Olive oil for frying

Clean and wash the squid. Mix together the flour and salt, coat the squid and fry in hot oil, turning constantly. When brown, remove from the pan and serve hot, garnished with slices of lemon.

Cod in lemon

½ kilo salted cod
1 dried onion
1 bunch spring onions
Dill
Parsley
2 tablesp. flour
1 lemon
Pepper
½ cup olive oil

Soak the cod overnight to remove salt. Heat the oil in a pan and saute the dried and spring onions. Add 2 cups of water and when it comes to the boil, add the dill and parsley. Meanwhile, prepare and wash the cod, cut into portions and add to the pan with seasoning for about 20 minutes. Dissolve the flour in a little water, lemon juice and broth from the fish and pour this into the pan, before bringing again to the boil.

Fried cod

½ kilo cod
1 egg
1 cup flour
Olive oil for frying

Soak the cod overnight in plenty of water. The following day wash well, clean and cut into portions. Make a batter by mixing together the flour, salt, beaten egg and a little water. Coat each piece of cod in batter and fry in very hot oil.

Pies

Chicken pie

1 chicken
½ kilo onions
3 eggs
½ cups milk
1 cups grated cheese
Salt - pepper - nutmeg
½ cup olive oil
10 pastry sheets

Wash the chicken and put on to boil. Add the onions cut in rings and the salt. When the chicken is tender, remove from the pan and leave the onions to continue boiling. Cut the chicken in pieces, discarding the skin and bones. When the stock with the onions has thickened, add the milk and the chicken, mix well and simmer. Remove the pan from the heat, add the eggs, grated cheese, and seasoning and stir well. Oil a baking tin and line with 7 pastry sheets, brushing each separately with oil. Spread filling over the pastry and cover with the remaining sheets, brushing each one and the top with oil. Mark the top of the pie into portions and bake in a moderate oven for about an hour.

Rice pie

½ kilo rice
9 eggs
½ kilo cheese
Pinch of salt
1 cup of olive oil
10 pastry sheets

Half boil the rice, drain and rinse with cold water. Place in a bowl adding salt, beaten eggs, grated cheese, and 3 spoonfuls of the oil. Mix well. Lay three of the pastry sheets in an oiled baking tin. Add a layer of filling and then alternatively 3 sheets of pastry and filling. Each pastry sheet must be brushed with oil. Score the top of the pie and bake in a pre-heated oven for about an hour.

Spinach pie

For the pastry
4 cups flour
1 cup water
1 cup olive oil
Pinch of salt
Juice and zest of half a lemon

For the filling
1 kilo spinach
2 leeks
4 spring onions
1 bunch dill
3 eggs
250 gr. feta
Salt - pepper
1 cup olive oil

Prepare, wash and cut up the spinach and leeks. Finely chop the dill and spring onions. Heat the oil and saute the onions, leeks, dill and spinach. Season and cook for a few minutes. Remove from the heat and when cold, add crumbled feta and the beaten eggs. Meanwhile make the pastry and roll out. Brush a baking tin with oil and line with half the pastry. Pour in the filling and cover with the rest of the pastry, marking the portions with a sharp knife. Brush the pie with a little oil and bake in a pre-heated oven for about 1 hour.

Leek pie

For the pastry
1 kilo flour
½ teasp. salt
2 cups water
3-4 tablesp. olive oil

For the filling
1 kilo leeks
6 eggs
300 gr. feta
2 cups milk
Salt - pepper
½ cups olive oil

Make the pastry and put on one side. Clean, wash and finely chop the leeks. Place in a bowl with the feta, beaten eggs, milk, oil and seasoning. Mix well. Roll out the pastry and lay half in an oiled baking tin. Pour in the filling and cover with the rest of the pastry. Brush with oil and score. Bake in a pre-heated oven for about an hour.

Cheese pie

For the pastry
2 cups flour
1 egg
5 tablesp. milk
½ teasp. salt
4 tablesp. olive oil

For the filling
½ kilo feta
3 eggs
1 cup milk
3 tablesp. flour or semolina
2 tablesp. olive oil

Knead the pastry and put on one side. Prepare the filling and then roll out the pastry, laying half in an oiled baking tin. Pour in the filling and cover with the rest of the pastry. Beat an egg and pour over the pastry. Bake in a pre-heated oven for about an hour.

Meat pie

For the pastry
2 cups water
1 cups olive oil
4-5 cups flour
1 teasp. vinegar
1 teasp. salt

For the filling
1 kilo minced beef
4 onions
1 cup grated Parmesan cheese
4 eggs
Salt - pepper - nutmeg
½ cup oil

Saute the finely chopped onion in hot oil. Add the minced beef, stirring constantly. Add a glass of water and seasoning and simmer. When the meat is tender, remove from heat, and when cold, add the Parmesan cheese, egg yolks and beaten egg whites and stir well. Roll out the pastry and line an oiled baking tin with half. Fill with the meat mixture and cover with the remaining pastry. Brush with oil, mark portions with a sharp knife, and bake in a pre-heated oven for about an hour.

Courgette pie

½ kilo courgettes
6 eggs
½ kilo feta cheese
Salt - pepper
½ cup olive oil
Pastry sheets

Wash, grate and season the courgettes. Add the grated feta, pepper and oil. Line an oiled baking tin with the pastry and spread on the filling. Bake in a pre-heated oven for about half an hour.

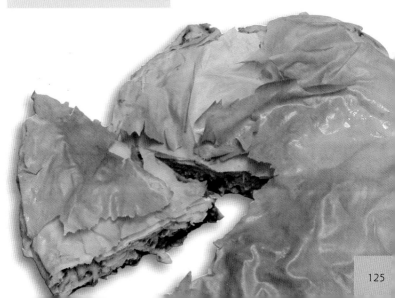

Desserts

Apple pie

5 cups flour
2 cups sugar
2 eggs
2 teasp. baking powder
1 cup crushed walnuts
Cinnamon
6-7 apples
Icing sugar
1 cup oil

Mix the oil well with one cup of sugar. Gradually add the eggs and the flour with the baking powder. The pastry must be quite stiff, almost crumbly.Grate the apples and mix with the remaining cup of sugar, the cinnamon and walnuts.Crumble half the pastry and spread in a baking dish. Pour on the apple mixture and on top of this the rest of the pastry. Bake for 30 - 40 minutes and when cold, sprinkle with icing sugar.

Kaltsounia

For the pastry
½ kilo flour
1 cup milk
1 tablesp. olive oil
Water as required

For the filling
½ kilo mizithra cheese
½ kilo anthotiro cheese
4 eggs
1-2 mint leaves
Sesame seeds

Make the pastry. Mix together the two cheeses, the eggs, and mint. Roll out the pastry and cut out circles with a pastry cutter or the top of a glass. Place a spoonful of filling on each circle, and fold over into half moon shapes. If preferred, the pastry can be cut into squares, the filling placed in the middle, and the four corners folded over, leaving the filling visible. Either way, place the kaltsounia on an oiled baking tray, brush with egg, and if desired, sprinkle with sesame seeds. Bake for about an hour in a moderate oven.

Walnut cake

1 cup olive oil
1 ½ cups sugar
6 eggs
1 cups milk
1 teasp. cinnamon
3-4 crushed cloves
3 cups crushed walnuts
½ kilo flour
2 teasp. baking powder

For the syrup
2 cups sugar
2 cups water
3 teasp. brandy

Beat the olive oil with the sugar in the mixer. Add the eggs, milk, walnuts, cinnamon, cloves, and finally the flour with the baking powder. Pour the mixture into an oiled baking tin and bake for about 45 minutes in a moderate oven. Make the syrup as follows: boil the water adding the sugar and brandy, stirring a little. Pour the hot syrup over the walnut cake.

Halva

1 cup semolina
½ cup olive oil
100 gr. crushed almonds
Cinnamon

For the syrup
1 ½ cups sugar
2 ½ cups water
Zest of one lemon

Heat the oil in a pan and add the semolina. Stir until the semolina turns golden brown. In another pan boil the water with the sugar, stirring for about five minutes until the sugar dissolves, and add the lemon zest. When the syrup is ready, gradually pour it into the pan containing the halva mixture and simmer until absorbed by the semolina. At the same time, add the almonds. Cover the pan with a clean tea towel and leave to cool. Serve in small bowls or on a serving dish sprinkled with cinnamon.

Kourabiethes (Christmas sweets)

1 cup flour
2 tablesp. sugar
3 tablesp. chopped walnuts
½ teasp. soda
½ lemon (juice and zest)
½ kilo icing sugar
Rosewater
2 cups oil

Mix the oil and sugar well together in a bowl. Add the soda, lemon, walnuts and finally the flour to make a stiff dough. Form the biscuits into whatever shape preferred and place on a lightly oiled baking tray. Bake in a pre-heated oven for about 40 minutes. When cooked, remove from the oven and sprinkle with a little rosewater. Sieve the icing sugar on to the biscuits and the sweets are ready.

Melomakarona (Christmas sweets)

6 cups flour
2 cups olive oil
1 cups icing sugar
1 cup milk
1 cup orange juice
1 teasp. orange zest
1 teasp. cinnamon
1 teasp. crushed cloves
½ cup crushed walnuts
1 teasp. soda
1 teasp. baking powder

Syrup

2 cups water
1 cup honey
1 cup sugar

Beat the oil well with the icing sugar. Add the zest and the soda dissolved in the orange juice, the cinnamon, cloves, walnuts and milk. Mix the baking powder with the flour and gradually add to the mixture, kneading to form a fairly soft dough. Shape small portions of the dough into round or oval biscuits and place on an oiled baking tin. Bake in a moderate oven for about 30 minutes. Meanwhile prepare the syrup as follows: boil the water in a pan adding the sugar and honey. When the syrup is ready and still hot, dip in each biscuit and remove immediately with a skimmer. Place on a serving dish and sprinkle with a mixture of crushed walnut, sesame seeds and cinnamon.

Raisin cake

1 kilo soft flour
½ kilo sugar
1 glass orange juice
1 glass water boiled
with a cinnamon stick
1 teasp. soda
1 teasp. ammonia
Zest of one lemon
1 cup chopped raisins
Crushed cloves
2 cups oil

Beat the oil and sugar well together. Dissolve the ammonia and soda in the orange juice and pour into the bowl with the oil and sugar. Add the cinnamon, cloves, lemon zest and raisins. Gradually add the flour and when the mixture is ready, pour into an oiled cake tin and bake in a pre-heated oven for about an hour.

Oil cake

4 ½ cups flour
1 cups sugar
1 ½ cups milk
2 eggs
1 teasp. baking powder
Juice and zest of one orange
1 vanilla powder
1 ½ cup oil

Beat the oil and sugar very well in a bowl. Gradually add the eggs, milk, orange juice and zest and the vanilla, and mix well. Add the baking powder to the flour and gradually pour into the mixture, stirring well. Oil a cake tin and pour in the mixture. Bake the cake in a pre-heated oven for about 45 minutes. The finished cake can be garnished with a little icing sugar if desired.

Olive oil cookies

4 cups soft flour
1 cup orange juice
3 cups sugar
1 teasp. ammonia
1 small cup raki
1 cinnamon stick
2 cups sesame seeds
3 cups olive oil

Beat the olive oil together with the orange juice, then add the sugar, the ammonia dissolved in the raki, and one cup of water boiled with the cinnamon stick. Gradually add the flour and knead to make a soft, pliable dough. Shape into long strips, roll in sesame seeds, cut into 10 - 12 cm lengths and form into an S-shape. Place on an oiled baking tray and bake for about an hour until golden brown.

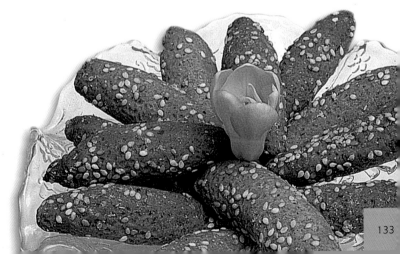

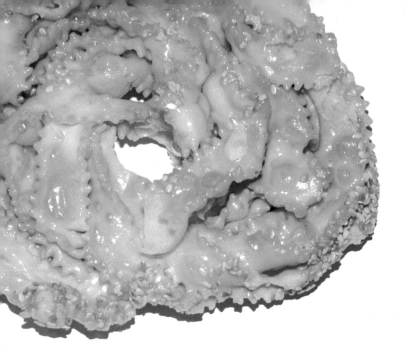

Fritters (Xerotigana)

1 kilo hard flour
½ cup sugar
1 cup raki
1 cup crushed walnuts
½ cup sesame seeds
Cinnamon
Honey
1 cup olive oil
Oil for frying

For the syrup
1 ½ cups sugar
2 ½ cups water

Mix together the oil, sugar, and raki, gradually adding the flour and water. The dough must be fairly stiff yet pliable, and when ready set on one side. After about an hour roll out the dough into thin sheets either in the traditional way or using a machine, and cut these into strips 3 cm wide and 30 - 40 cm long. Heat the oil in a frying pan and taking one strip at a time, hold one end with a fork, place in hot oil, and turn the fork so as to shape a kind of nest. If preferred, the nests can be formed on the table and then fried. When golden brown, the fritter is ready. Remove from pan and place on kitchen paper to soak up any excess oil. Prepare the syrup and when the fritters go cold, dip them one by one into the syrup for 1-2 minutes. Place on a serving dish and garnish with honey, walnuts, sesame seeds and cinnamon.

Mizithra pies with honey

For the pastry
1 kilo flour
2 eggs
½ teasp. soda
1 cup water
1/3 cup oil

For the filling
1 kilo mizithra cheese
2 eggs
1 teasp. cinnamon
A little finely chopped mint
Honey

Beat the eggs and add oil. Mix well and add the water and soda with the flour to make a stiff dough. Leave on one side wrapped in a towel and prepare the filling by mixing the mizithra with the eggs, cinnamon and mint. Roll out the dough using either a rolling pin or machine, and with a pastry cutter or a glass, cut out circles. Place a teaspoonful of filling on each circle and fold over to form a half-moon shape. Heat the oil in a frying pan and fry the little pies. Serve hot with honey.

Mizithra pies from Sfakia

For the pastry
½ kilo flour
1 egg
3 tablesp. oil

For the filling
½ kilo mizithra cheese
Cinnamon
Honey

Place the flour in a bowl, adding the beaten egg, oil, and as much water as needed to make a moderately soft pastry. Prepare the filling by mixing together all the ingredients. Divide the dough into small balls and roll each out into a circle the size of a side plate. Spread on each a little filling, sprinkle with cinnamon and fold over the pastry. Lightly press with the fingers to flatten the pie. Fry one by one in a frying pan without oil or with just a drop, turning constantly so as not to burn. Pour over honey and serve.

Raising Pie

1 kilo flour
1 ½ cups sugar
½ cup orange juice
Juice and zest of one lemon
½ cup lye
1 teasp. soda
Cinnamon
Cloves
1 small glass
brandy or liqueur
Chopped raisins
½ kilo olive oil

Place in a bowl the oil, sugar, orange juice, lemon zest, lye, brandy, cinnamon and cloves and beat well for about half an hour. Mix the soda with the lemon juice, add to the mixture, followed gradually by the flour, When the dough is stiff enough to be kneaded, roll out and cut into circles with a pastry cutter or top of a glass. Place on each piece a spoonful of chopped raisins and fold over into a half moon shape. Place on an oiled baking tray and bake in a pre-heated oven.

Ravani

800 gr. rice
1 kilo sugar
1 cup chopped almonds
Cinnamon
Cloves
1 cup oil

Boil and mash the rice. Boil 2 litres of water in a pan with the sugar, and then add half the oil, the rice and the almonds. Stir until smooth and thick. Pour into an oiled baking tin and sprinkle with cinnamon. Score in pieces, stick a clove in each and bake in the oven for about an hour.

Notes

Notes

Notes

Notes

Notes

Notes

Notes